Peck, Hen, Peck!
and Ben's Pet

By Jill Atkins

Illustrated by
Barbara Vagnozzi

The Letter 'k'

Trace the lower and upper case letter with a finger. Sound out the letter.

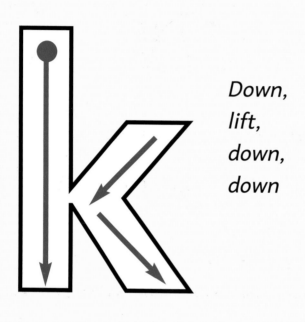

*Down,
lift,
down,
down*

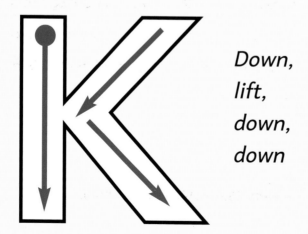

*Down,
lift,
down,
down*

Peck, Hen, Peck!
and Ben's Pet

'Peck, Hen, Peck!' and 'Ben's Pet'
An original concept by Jill Atkins
© Jill Atkins

Illustrated by Barbara Vagnozzi

Published by MAVERICK ARTS PUBLISHING LTD
Studio 3A, City Business Centre, 6 Brighton Road,
Horsham, West Sussex, RH13 5BB
© Maverick Arts Publishing Limited May 2017
+44 (0)1403 256941

A CIP catalogue record for this book is available at the British Library.

ISBN 978-1-84886-248-7

www.maverickbooks.co.uk

Pink

This book is rated as: Pink Band (Guided Reading)
This story is decodable at Letters and Sounds Phase 2.

Some words to familiarise:

hen   bag   Tom

High-frequency words:

on put at his in the of

Tips for Reading 'Peck, Hen, Peck!'

- Practise the words listed above before reading the story.

- If the reader struggles with any of the other words, ask them to look for sounds they know in the word. Encourage them to sound out the words and help them read the words if necessary.

- After reading the story, ask the reader ask how the hen managed to escape.

Fun Activity

Discuss where you think the hen may have gone.

Peck, Hen, Peck!

Tom puts the hen in his bag.

Tom puts the bag on his back.

The hen pecks at the bag.

The hen gets out of the bag.

Run,
run,
run!

Oh no! The hen runs away.

The Letter P

Trace the lower and upper case letter with a finger. Sound out the letter.

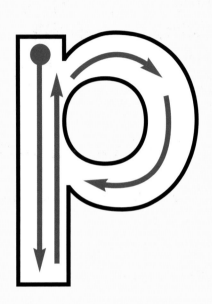

Down,
up,
around

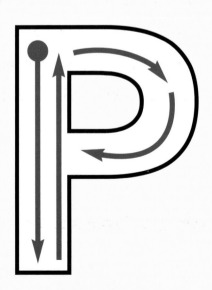

Down,
up,
around

Some words to familiarise:

Ben   rat   rabbit

High-frequency words:

has a is it

Tips for Reading 'Ben's Pet'

- Practise the words listed above before reading the story.

- If the reader struggles with any of the other words, ask them to look for sounds they know in the word. Encourage them to sound out the words and help them read the words if necessary.

- After reading the story, ask the reader what animal they thought was in the box.

Fun Activity

Discuss favourite animals and what pets the reader would like.

Ben's Pet

Ben has a pet.

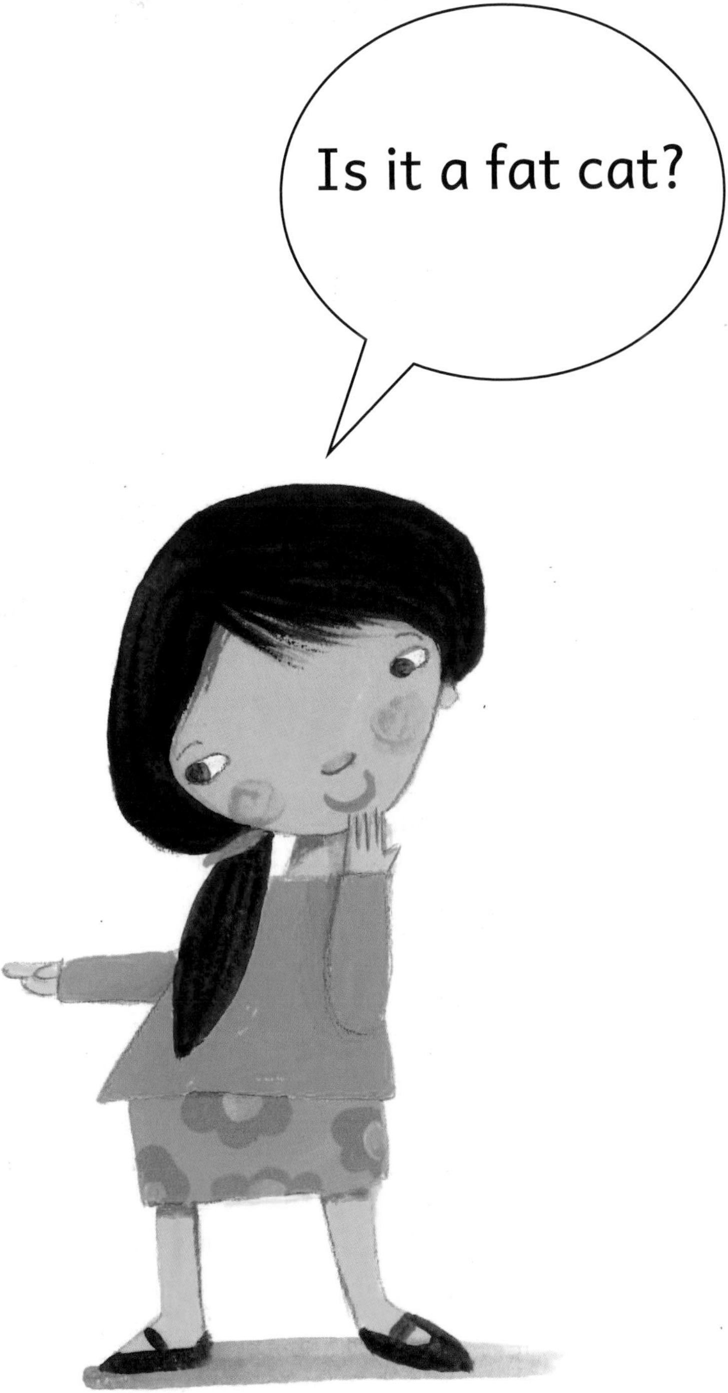
Is it a fat cat?

Pink

Red (End of Yr R)

Yellow

Blue

Green

Orange

Turquoise (End of Yr 1)

Purple

Gold

White (End of Yr 2)

Lime

Book Bands for Guided Reading

The Institute of Education book banding system is made up of twelve colours, which reflect the level of reading difficulty. The bands are assigned by taking into account the content, the language style, the layout and phonics.

Children learn at different speeds but the colour chart shows the levels of progression with the national expectation shown in brackets. To learn more visit the IoE website: www.ioe.ac.uk.

All of these books have been book banded for guided reading to the industry standard and edited by a leading educational consultant.

For more titles visit: www.maverickbooks.co.uk/early-readers